LETTERS HOME
from
PERU

Lisa Halvorsen

BLACKBIRCH PRESS, INC.

WOODBRIDGE, CONNECTICUT

Published by Blackbirch Press, Inc.
260 Amity Road
Woodbridge, CT 06525

©2000 by Blackbirch Press, Inc.
First Edition

e-mail: staff@blackbirch.com
Web site: www.blackbirch.com

Printed in Singapore

10 9 8 7 6 5 4 3 2 1

All photographs ©Corel Corporation.

Library of Congress Cataloging-in-Publication Data
Halvorsen, Lisa.
Peru / by Lisa Halvorsen.
    p.   cm. — (Letters home from . . .)
Includes index.
Summary: Describes some of the sights and experiences on a trip to Peru, including visits to
Lima, the walled city of Cuzco, and Machu Picchu.
ISBN 1-56711-414-8 (alk. paper)
1. Peru—Description and travel—Juvenile literature. [1. Peru—Description and travel.]
I. Title.
  F3425 .H35 2000
918.504'633—dc21
                                                                           00-009008

TABLE OF CONTENTS

Arrival in . . .

Lima

Here we are in Peru, the Land of the Incas. I can't wait to discover the mysteries Peru has to offer and to meet the Peruvian people.

Peru is located on the west central coast of South America. In size, it's slightly smaller than the state of Alaska. Peru is divided into three distinct regions—the coast, mountains, and rain forest.

Nearly half of its 26 million people are descended from the earlier Indian cultures that once lived in Peru. Spanish and Quechua are the official languages.

Lima

I read in my guidebook that Lima was founded in 1535 by Francisco Pizarro, a Spanish conquistador. He named it Cuidad de los Reyes, which is Spanish for "City of the Kings." The name was later changed to Lima. The population of 6.5 million makes it the largest city in Peru. It is also the capital. Lima is on the coast where the Rimac River meets the Pacific Ocean.

We began our walking tour of Lima at the Plaza de Armas (main square). The oldest part of this plaza is the bronze fountain built in 1650. The National Cathedral in the square has many beautiful religious artifacts. This cathedral had to be completely rebuilt after a horrible earthquake in 1746.

National Cathedral, Plaza de Armas

Knocker, National Cathedral

Changing of the guard, Government Palace

Marching guards, Government Palace

We passed by the Government Palace, just in time to see the changing of the guard. What a spectacular sight! This is the official residence of the country's president. It also houses his offices and those of his staff.

Later, we visited the Church of San Francisco, completed in 1674. I thought the catacombs were the best part. The remains of more than 70,000 people are buried here. At the Museum of the Inquisition, we explored early dungeons and torture chambers. This building was the headquarters for the Spanish Inquisition for 250 years, beginning in 1570. The Spanish Inquisition was an attempt by the Catholic Church to force people to convert to Catholicism.

Lima

Our guide took us to Palacio Torre Tagle. This elaborate colonial mansion was built in 1735. Today it houses the foreign ministry. You can't go inside, but you can peek into the courtyard and patio. We saw a 16th-century carriage with its own bathroom! Our guide also showed us the bridge over the Rimac River. The 530-foot-long Puente de Piedra was built in the 17th century using egg whites! The builders mixed thousands of egg whites into the mortar to make it stronger!

Balcony, Palacio Torre Tagle

Interior patio, Torre Tagle

Street vendors

Plaza San Martín

We walked from the Plaza de Armas along the Jirón de la Unión to the modern Plaza San Martín. Along the way we passed many street performers and vendors selling flowers, fruit, clothing, jewelry, and other items. We also saw many beggars. Many Peruvians from the highlands and other rural areas come to Lima hoping to find work, but not all of them do.

Nazca and the Peruvian Coast

Today we flew over Nazca, the site of one of the world's greatest ancient mysteries—the Nazca Lines. Our pilot explained that thousands of years ago an ancient Indian race called the Nazcas (A.D. 200-700) made huge sand drawings in the Pampa de San José. The lines were scratched into the hard crust of this sunbaked plain.

Some people believe that the pictures form a large astronomical calendar. Others think the Nazcas invented a hot air balloon, and this was their airfield. Not everyone is convinced that humans did this work. Some say the lines were made by visitors from outer space!

Desert plateau near Nazca

Pelicans near the Peruvian coast

Candelabra of the Andes

At different heights you can see different pictures. We saw a huge spider, a hummingbird, and a condor. My favorite was the 300-foot monkey with its long, spiraling tail.

Our pilot told us he had one more surprise for us. He began to fly toward the ocean. Suddenly he turned back toward land. There, in front of us, carved into the cliff, was a giant, branched candlestick. He said that the Candelabra of the Andes, as it is known, is 840 feet high. The cliff carving is in Paracas, a large nature preserve with wildlife. It includes Chilean flamingos, Inca terns, Peruvian pelicans, and sea lions.

Arequipa

We continued down the coast to Arequipa in the Andes Mountains. It is called "the white city" because of the sillar—light-colored volcanic stone—that's used in construction of the buildings. It is Peru's second-largest city with a population of 635,000. It is also surrounded by mountains, including the 19,089-foot-tall volcano El Misti.

I read that Arequipa was founded by Francisco Pizarro five years after he established Lima. Today it is a commercial center, and the chief industry is the grading and packing of llama wool.

We visited the Santa Catalina Convent, which was built in late 1500s. It's like a city within a city. It has many buildings, a library, gardens, and squares with fountains. It was once one of the largest convents in the world.

Woman weaving cloth

Peruvian llamas

Colca Canyon

From Arequipa we traveled through the highlands to Colca Canyon. At 11,500 feet deep, Colca Canyon is one of the deepest canyons in the Americas—even deeper than the Grand Canyon! From a lookout along the rim—called Cruz del Condor—we spotted a pair of Andean condors. They were gliding on thermal air currents that rise from the floor of the 36-mile-long canyon. This rare bird is the largest flighted raptor in the world. It has a ten-foot wingspan!

Herdsman playing flute

Highland boy

Andes Mountains

The Andes are the longest mountain range in the world, and second-highest after the Himalayas. They extend for about 5,500 miles along the west coast of South America. The Peruvian Andes are made up of several cordilleras, or mountain chains. The highest peak is the 22,205-foot-high Huascarán in Cordillera Blanca. Even though the Andes straddle the equator, many of the higher peaks are covered with snow year-round.

Mountain dwellings

Andes Mountains

The high
Andes

Llamas and
herders

The Andean slopes are rocky and steep. But that didn't stop the people from finding a way to farm the land. They have constructed terraces by building stone walls 8 to 15 feet high and filling them with soil from the river valleys. These terraces were built one on top of the other, with as many as 100 terraces on a single slope. Irrigation systems provide water for the crops. Herders also tend flocks of llamas and alpacas for their wool and meat.

Lake Titicaca

The train trip from Arequipa to Puno on the shores of Lake Titicaca was very long. But it was worth it to see the highest navigable lake in the world! Lake Titicaca is 120 miles long and 50 miles wide. It sits on a high plateau, 12,500 feet above sea level. Incan myths tell of Manco Capac and Mama Ocllo, children of the sun, who arose from the lake to start a new empire.

The women here weave the soft wool of llamas and alpacas into colorful blankets and clothing. They dress in the traditional clothing of the highlands—a wide skirt called a pollera. Most wear a shawl around their shoulders, fastened with a tupu (large metal pin), and a felt bowler hat. The men wear woolen ponchos over a shirt and trousers.

Lake Titicaca

Reed boats on Lake Titicaca

Terraced farms on Taquile Island

We traveled by boat to the floating islands. These islands are home to about 300 Uros Indians. They are built on totora reeds. The Indians use these reeds to construct their houses and boats.

Last night we stayed on Taquile, the island of weavers. There are no hotels here, but the people let visitors stay overnight in their homes. The house where we stayed had no electricity. Water for washing was hauled up from the lake. That evening, after a meal of lake trout and boiled potatoes, we attended a fiesta in the main plaza. While everyone danced, local musicians played guitars and the panpipe, a traditional flutelike instrument.

Cuzco

The next day, back on shore, we hired a taxi to take us to Juliaca. There, we caught a plane to Cuzco. The first thing we did when we got to Cuzco was to take a nap. That's so we didn't get soroche (altitude sickness). Cuzco is the ancient Incan capital. It is located on an altiplano (high plateau) at an altitude of 11,500 feet. Less oxygen in the air at this high elevation makes it hard to breathe. You can also get a bad headache or an upset stomach. Resting helps, as does drinking maté—tea made of dried coca leaves.

Rooftops of Cuzco

Mother and daughter

Stairway street

Street corner near cathedral

The walled city of Cuzco is the oldest continuously inhabited city in the western hemisphere. It is located in the Valley of the Huatanay River in the southeastern Andes. At the entrance to the city is a gigantic statue of Pachacutec Inca. He was a 15th-century ruler, mighty warrior, and great empire builder. We climbed inside the statue to an observation deck for our first glimpse of the city.

Did you know that the original city was laid out in the shape of a puma? Our guide also told us that when the Spaniards conquered the city, they built their churches and houses on top of the Incan walls!

Cuzco

The Cathedral in Cuzco, with its elaborate stonework and Spanish-style architecture, was really impressive. It was built on the site of the palace of the Inca ruler Viracocha. It was begun in the mid-16th century and took nearly 100 years to complete. Inside are 400 paintings, including one of the Last Supper with Jesus and his disciples enjoying a meal of cuy. That's roasted guinea pig, a traditional dish of Cuzco.

I don't think I'd like cuy, but I have tried other native dishes like ceviche (raw fish in lemon juice), ají de gallina (shredded chicken in a spicy cheese sauce), and purple corn pudding. Tropical fruits like mango, papaya, and chirimoya (custard apple) are really delicious.

Courtyard

Cathedral

Vendors in marketplace

Marketplace

We wandered through the Church of Santo Domingo. It was built on top of the Temple of the Sun God (Coricancha). This temple had halls dedicated to the moon, the stars, the rainbow, thunder, and lightning.

On Sunday we caught the local bus to Pisac for market day. The market was crowded—and noisy—as everyone bargained for goods. Everywhere I looked, I saw mounds of potatoes, plantains (bananas), avocados, and other locally grown fruits and vegetables spread out on blankets.

I was amazed by the many different kinds of potatoes. Some were yellow. Others were brown, purple, red, or blue. Peruvian potato production dates back to the time of the Incan empire (A.D. 1400–1532). The Incas planted more than 200 varieties on the slopes of the Andes.

Anta Valley

We took the morning train to Machu Picchu, the "Lost City of the Incas." The trip started slowly as our train zigzagged up the steep slope of Picchu Mountain on the outskirts of Cuzco.

Then the train descended into the Sacred Valley of the Incas. We passed through tiny villages before reaching the Anta plains. This is a major agricultural area. I saw men and women farming fields of potatoes, maize (corn), and wheat by hand. Children played outside their mud-brick homes with thatched grass roofs. In the distance, I saw 20,574-foot-high snow-covered Mt. Salcantay. The Incas considered it a sacred mountain. Its name means "maker of awesome skies."

Train along Anta River

Thatched cottages

Urubamba River

At Huarocondo, the train tracks began following the Urubamba River. The Incas believed that this sacred river flowed into the heavens where it became part of the Milky Way. Peru is crisscrossed with many rivers. The biggest is the Amazon, which has its source in the Peruvian Andes.

Near Pisac, the winding Urubamba River flows in a straight line. That's because the Incas formed that section into a canal to irrigate the surrounding farmland. But for most of its 450 miles, the fast-moving river twists and turns, eventually flowing into the faraway Amazon. This river is popular with white-water rafters from around the world.

Gorge of the Urubamba

Urubamba River

Machu Picchu

During the four-hour train trip, I read about Machu Picchu. I learned that it was discovered in 1911 by Professor Hiram Bingham of Yale University. He was searching for Vilcambamba, the fortified city where the Incas hid from the conquistadors. Although later expeditions proved that this was not Vilcambamba, it's still a spectacular find. The Incas abandoned this site long before the Spaniards came to Peru, but no one knows why.

From the Puente Ruinas train station, we hopped on a bus to the ruins. It took us 30 minutes to make our way up the steep Hiram Bingham Highway. The Incas built their city between two rugged peaks, Machu Picchu (old peak) and Huayna Picchu (young peak), overlooking the Urubamba river canyon.

Machu Picchu

Machu Picchu

Door of Sun Temple

The Inca Fortress

Our guide met us at the entrance of the complex. He told us that no one knows for sure why Machu Picchu was built. It may have been a retreat for Incan royalty. Or it could have been an agricultural settlement, or a place where religious ceremonies were held. It might have been a refuge for acllas and mamacunas, chosen women of the Incas. Acllas were young girls selected for special training in religion, weaving, and cooking. The mamacunas were their teachers.

Machu Picchu

The city is divided into three sections—agricultural, residential, and religious. The different parts are connected by stairways carved out of stone by hand. Our guide led us through the agricultural area first. That's where the Incas grew crops on irrigated terraces.

I took lots of pictures, including some of the grassy central court, which separates the urban and religious parts. Our guide showed us the Sacred Plaza with its large sundial and temples to the sun, moon, and stars. We also saw the Temple of the Sun—the only round building at Machu Picchu—and the Temple of the Three Windows, a three-sided building.

Sun Temple, Machu Picchu

Central area, Machu Picchu

Orchid

Interior, Main Temple

At the ruins we talked to some people who had hiked the Inca Trail to Machu Picchu. It took them four days to walk many miles over the rough, steep lands through jungle and cloud forest.

The trail and the ruins are part of the Machu Picchu Historical Sanctuary. This was established as a nature preserve in 1981 to protect the ruins, plants, and animals. Many endangered animal species live in this jungle, like the spectacled bear and dwarf deer. It's also home to ocelots, Andean foxes, and hundreds of butterfly and bird species, including the bright orange cock-of-the-rock, Peru's national bird. More than 90 different species of orchids grow in the jungle.

Ancient Ruins

Back in Cuzco, we hired a guide to shoe zigzag walls represent the teeth of the sacred puma. It was here that Pizarro was killed in battle. After the Spaniards won, they destroyed the fortress, using llamas to help topple the structure.

We also went to Tambo Machay, built at the site of some sacred springs. Our guide told us that the Incas thought that water was a source of life. Their aqueduct system still brings water to the baths once used by Incan royalty.

Incan terraced land

Ruins at Chan Chan

Chan Chan

The Incas were not the only early Indian culture in Peru. According to my guidebook, the Chimús were also there. They were fishermen and farmers who lived in Peru from A.D. 1000 to 1470. Today you can visit the ruins of Chan Chan, capital of their ancient empire, on the coast near Trujillo. It is the largest adobe city ever built. It had 10,000 buildings on 15 square miles!

In 1987, archaeologists discovered a burial tomb of a Moche king at Sipán to the north. The Moches lived in Peru 1,200 years before the Incas. Nearby, at Túcume, work is underway to uncover 28 pyramids hidden for years by desert sands.

Amazon Basin

Last night we flew to Iquitos, the gateway to the Amazon Basin. This city of 350,000 people sits on the banks of the Upper Amazon River. It was once the center of a booming rubber industry. Many of the houses here are built on stilts.

About three-fifths of Peru is jungle or rain forest. It is very hot and humid. From December to March it rains every day. More than half of all the world's plant and animal species, including one-fifth of all its birds, are found in the Amazon Basin. More than 80,000 different plants have been identified. Many are used for food, perfumes, and medicines.

Nanay River

Capybara

Parrot

This morning we visited the floating market in Iquitos. Then we boarded the boat that will be our home for the next few days. As we traveled down the river, pink freshwater dolphins swam in our wake. Once we left the city behind, we began to see wildlife. Our captain pointed out a capybara and lots of colorful parrots along the shore. He also said we should spot caimans, and if we are lucky, giant river otters and anacondas—the world's largest snakes. Many of these animals are found nowhere else on Earth.

I don't know what I've liked best about Peru—seeing the wildlife, meeting the people, or learning about the ancient cultures. From the coastal plains to the Andes and the Amazon rain forest, Peru certainly has been an exciting place to explore!

Glossary

Adobe brick made of sun-dried mud and straw.

Aqueduct a large pipe or canal made for bringing water from a distant source.

Archaeologist someone who studies the remains, such as buildings, pottery, and works of art of past civilizations.

Caiman an alligator-type reptile found in Central and South America.

Capybara a large aquatic rodent, resembling a guinea pig.

Coca a shrub in the jungles of the eastern slopes of the Andes Mountains.

Conquistador the Spanish word for conqueror.

Mortar a mixture of cement or sand and water used in construction.

Quechua one of the early human cultures who lived north of Cuzco and were friends of the Incas.

Theory an idea or guess about how or why something might have been done.

For More Information

Books

Blue, Rose. Corinne J. Naden. *Andes Mountains* (Wonders of the World). Chatham, NJ: Raintree/Steck Vaughn, 1994.

Landau, Elaine. *Peru* (True Book). Danbury, CT: Children's Press, 2000.

Lyle, Garry. *Peru* (Major World Nations). New York, NY: Chelsea House, 1998.

Sayer, Chloe. *The Incas* (The Ancient World). Chatham, NJ: Raintree/Steck Vaughn, 1998.

Web Site
The World Factbook Page on Peru

This Central Intelligence Agency web site provides much information on Peru's geography, government, population, and economy— www.odci.gov/cia/publications/factbook/pe.html.

Index